Design Your Dream Life

Your ultimate motivational book for success.

Live the life you deserve and want.

The plan to design and live your dream life.

To discover your true passion in life
To start uncovering what is important to you
To awaken your soul's desire
To be happy and fulfilled
To reach your goal in life
To have total happiness in the palm of your hands

Follow this workbook step by step and find your dream life.

DesignYourDreamLife.com

Design Your Dream Life

Designing the Life of Your Dreams

Nothing is Impossible

Play the Possibility Game and Win

Mera Lord

Writers Club Press
San Jose New York Lincoln Shanghai

Design Your Dream Life

Writers Club Press
an imprint of iUniverse, Inc.

For information address:
iUniverse, Inc.
5220 S. 16th St., Suite 200
Lincoln, NE 68512
www.iuniverse.com

ISBN: 0-595-20990-4

Printed in the United States of America

To my great help in life, my husband, Bob.

Thank you for being there for me.

Thank you for all the attention, help, honesty, laughs, kindness, and support that you have always shown.

You believed in me when life's challenges were too heavy to carry.

And to my children Nina and Sebastian, to believe in themselves and design their own dream lives.

Epigraph

This book is also dedicated to you, the reader.

I want you to believe in yourself and know deep in your heart that there is always a way out. There is a winning plan and all you have to do is to want it.

Remember this: when the calling is within your heart, you cannot possibly be defeated.

Contents

Foreword

What makes this book different than other motivational books?

The answer is, not only this book will motivate your thoughts, but it will also lead you to happiness and help you find balance in all areas of your life.

I have had a wonderful life, with my share of reality. I have had my taste of all seasons, happiness, sadness, difficulties, confusion, hopes, and dreams.

I have always searched to find the answer to the meaning of life. As a young child, I had my share of difficulties, which forced me to search for answers and fight back. As a result, I studied psychology in college. With the hopes of helping others to succeed.

I have discovered that I am an excellent listener and people are drawn to me like a butterfly to a light. I could spot their needs and solve their problems like magic. But yet, I was struggling to find answers for my everyday difficulties. Maybe this was an asset for me, to search for the answers myself, and be able to help my clients directly.

I found something in common with all my clients' problems. It didn't matter what specifically their problems were, they didn't know where to start, or how to resolve them. They were lost in their sadness so much they couldn't see the light in the middle of the darkness to free themselves. They couldn't see the whole picture.

You have to see your life as a maze. There will be dead-ends, road-blocks, tunnels, mountains, oceans, and many more obstacles placed in your way to success and total happiness.

What are you going to do?

Are you going to stay in one place in times of roadblocks or go back to where you have started?

Are you going to find a way to reach your destination?

If a child was working on a maze, wouldn't you help him to find a way out? Could you convince a frustrated child that there was a way out from start to finish?

Here you will discover the simple method to focus on the complete picture of your life, to follow the road, and get to the finish line at your pace, and the way you want.

Chapter 1—Reach Your Highest Dreams

I want you to achieve your highest dreams and feel fulfilled in life.

I want you to see nothing is impossible.

There is always a way out.

There is happiness and achievement waiting for you. The only thing you need to do is believe, follow the map, know the rules, and just play the game.

This book has been uniquely designed to work with your thoughts and show you the way to have it all.

This is a workbook to lead you to the ultimate achievement in your life.

A guide to finding and living your dreams.

Achieve your highest

Fight for a better future. What will you do if you are not happy or you feel there is something missing in your life? This is the time to get up and explore.

See all the possibilities that are awaiting you. You have the power to create the life of your dreams. Create your own luck by turning your dreams into reality.

Keep in mind to never quit. To achieve success is to stay focused on your goals. Never allow obstacles to take your dreams away.

It is a new beginning. You always have a choice. You can find a way out if your desire is higher than your fear. In the pursuit of achieving an abundance life you need to work at it. You need to dream it, plan it, fight the obstacles, and be highly resourceful.

Your hard work will be rewarded. Be certain about your faith and your vision of the future. This is a powerful door to open.

Run a successful life by planning your way.

Here is the plan and how to get what you want.

Do you believe in your dream?

I was talking to a very close friend one day. We have known each other since childhood. We always stay in touch and talk about everything. She is very successful in her career, but her romantic life wasn't going the way she wanted it to. So she made up her mind not to try, or worse yet, not to give romance another chance. She asked me if she should quit or she should keep on trying to find the right person. She had a lot of questions.

Is there going to be a right person?

Is it an illusion or fantasy that we make for ourselves?

I don't want it to be made up. I want it to be real. Which is right?

Do we make things happen or is it set for us?

Why don't things sometimes work out the way we want them to?

There are lots of emotional questions and uncertainties when you are in stress or facing obstacles. At the time of stress you may not be able to see the answers clearly. You would not know what to do, or which road to take.

The answer is within your question. The answer is here and now.

The Answer is here

As long as you have questions, it means there is a *desire*.

When there is a desire, there is a *dream*.

When there is a dream, there should be a belief.

You should believe in the reality. There are ways to make your dream a reality.

All you need to do is to learn the skills, and use them to accomplish your mission.

Who would have believed that one day there would be television, telephone, computer, and much more?

There are the ones who dreamed it.

Those who dreamed it, those who believed it, and didn't let the non-believers touch their dream or get in the way of their focus.

The non-believers laughed in their faces.

Is it going to be a box you see moving pictures in?

Can someone talk to another and hear them from the other side of the world?

I think you need to rest in the mental hospital, and ha, ha, ha, the laughs non-believers had.

The non-believer's attitude still exits even today. I get a laugh from my own family anytime I move into a new territory, or expand my horizons. My feelings get hurt, especially when it is coming from family and loved ones. But, this is life; they don't know any better. They are not to blame because they do not see the errs of their way. They just need to learn and respect other people's point of view.

The reality of life is no matter which road you take there will be road-blocks. The only way to succeed is to stay focused and in line with your dreams and passions in life.

You are the one living your life. You are the one who has to be satisfied with your decisions.

And yes, there are Televisions, radios, telephones, movies, cars, and many more things. And yes, there are successful and happy people.

How hard can it be for you and I to dream of having the best career, family, love, and have all the happiness we want to achieve in our lives?

How difficult can it be? It is not hard at all. It is as easy as playing a game. Get to know the rules and get smarter every time you play it.

Lead your life toward success and ultimate happiness.

What is your passion?

Were you always like this? How do you describe your personality, vision, strengths, and attitude toward life?

What is your ultimate goal?

Do you truly understand yourself?

What is your mission?

Search your heart and soul.

You don't need to hide behind walls. Forget about the boundaries and what others might think. You need to keep your focus on yourself and on what is important to you in achieving your life's dream.

Be clear and stand up for what is important to you, not what is popular or important to others. Your focus should be on how to lead your life.

You need to take a position, see where you stand, accept the challenges, fight for good, stand up for your beliefs, and everything else will follow.

Plan your life.

Lead Your Life

- **Believe in the cause**

  If you don't believe with all your heart and soul, then you are not the leader of your life.

- **Integrity**

  The power is in your personality, courage, intelligence, true beliefs and caring.

- **Noble cause**

  Stand for something greater than yourself.

- **Fight back**

  You will always win when you fight back in life.

- **Push your limits**

  If you are not pushing yourself every day to go forward, then your life will lead you.

- **Endure pain**

  Get to know your limits, your abilities, and the power of achievements.

- **Help others**

  Help others in any possible way you can, but remember you come first.

- **Handle pressure**

  The first rule of survival is to know that you are able to handle pressure under any situation. Handling pressure does not mean to runaway from the situation or ignoring it. But, it is to find solutions and get back to the main road.

- **Guidance**

  Using guidance is to stay focused on your vision. Use mentors and resources.

I am Worthy

Build up your self-esteem, learn to love yourself, and claim full independence. This is very important on the road to achieve your dream life.

The first step is to respect yourself. No matter what other people think of you or about you.

You must believe in yourself. Put aside other people's opinions of you. Never assume other people's thoughts about what you do or what you have done.

Create a positive reality. Use your mind to eliminate negatives and to concentrate on the positive side of life.

Write your thoughts.

I am worthy because:

_____

_____

_____

_____

_____

_____

_____

_____

_____

_____

_____

_____

_____

_____

_____

_____

_____

_____

_____

_____

_____

_____

_____

_____

You must learn not to be adversely affected by criticism. Do not let criticism effect the part of you that respects you.

When you respect yourself, when you believe in yourself, when you know you are on the right track of doing good, then you can stand up to the negativity that might be brought to you from outside sources.

When you feel dowdy, no-good, unsuccessful, fat, ugly, or anything negative, it is easy for the slightest everyday mishap to get reinforced. Get rid of any negative habit cycle thinking.

List your negative thinking habits.

The ways I can detect and get rid of negativity.

_____

_____

_____

_____

_____

_____

_____

_____

_____

_____

_____

_____

_____

_____

_____

_____

_____

_____

_____

_____

_____

_____

_____

Treat Yourself Well

Practice and learn the good habits of loving, and respecting yourself, by saying;

> "I am okay"
>
> "I am all right"
>
> "I am a good person"
>
> "I am a nice person"
>
> "I am a person who really counts"

Do the things that make you feel like you really count. Find things that make you and others happy.

Have a life plan. Create one. Start with your dream, expand on it, and do research on how to get where you want to be.

You need to start feeling positive, becoming positive, be more self-aware, and more interested in the world around you.

Never hold yourself back. Express your thoughts and your feelings. Everyone is different; everyone might have an opinion, respect other's opinions, as you respect your own.

Pamper yourself and work toward making yourself feel good about you. If you don't do it, no one else will do it for you. Loving yourself is the first step to being able to love other people.

Take control of your life, your decision-making, and your independence.

Even if your circumstances do not allow you to be totally independent, you can still achieve certain amount of independence. Manage to have at least one or two hours a day to spend by yourself, thinking on your dreams, and making plans.

Becoming independent is the most rewarding and positive thing anyone can do to take control of his or her life.

Make yourself the center of your life to fully love and respect yourself. Then the success and happiness of your life will expand to reach your family and friends.

List the things you need to do, to treat yourself personally and emotionally better.

_____

_____

_____

_____

_____

_____

_____

_____

_____

_____

_____

_____

_____

_____

_____

_____

_____

_____

_____

_____

_____

_____

_____

Chapter 2—In Search of Happiness

Total happiness can be reached and it will be yours to keep.

- Find out what is really important to you and concentrate on it.

- Keep journals. Write down the things you would like to achieve

- Write down things in term of wants. I want to do this and that. I want to be there.

- Make decisions on how to get closer to your true desires. Everything starts with one step at a time and act as if it is there for you.

- Act on it as if it has already happened. (Example: I want to be successful. Work on it little by little, step by step. While working to get where you want to be just say: I am successful. I am successful.)

- Finding the right balance with all the things that matter to you such as family, career, children, health, fitness, friends, your past, and your future.

- Knowing what to do in daily life and make long-term plans for what you would like to do, and where you would like to be in the near and far future.

Your inner vision will lead the way.

The first move is to call on your inner vision.

What do you want from your life?

If it weren't for money, time, or society, what would you really love to do with your life?

What gives you a feeling of self-respect and fulfillment?

When you concentrate on your dreams, you ignite the flame of energy behind every positive achievement.

The ability to believe that you hold destiny in your own hands.

Have concrete vision and clear view of your future. Believe in possibilities and your passion will inspire you to make the effort. Make the effort to be what you dream to have or be.

No matter what obstacles you had in your life, you can choose to be a winner of your true destiny. Plan and make your life what you have always dreamed of. It is never too late.

What you need is the desire to learn how to be joyous, fulfilled, and a winner.

Are you ready to have it all?

What do you want out of life? Is it money, luxury, exciting people or wonderful companionship?

What will your choices be?

List all your choices and let's turn fantasies into reality.

_____

_____

_____

_____

_____

_____

_____

_____

_____

_____

_____

_____

_____

_____

_____

_____

_____

_____

Realize your dreams

and

learn how to go for them.

Time

As a winner you have to realize your time is limited, therefore you need to be selective in your choices. Select and pursue the objectives, which are real and fit to your standards.

Action

You have to find your own niche.

You have to take active actions, taking many different directions, failing and trying new avenues until you discover your true niche.

Obstacles

Winners believe no matter how unfortunate their training or childhood was, they can positively change the course of their lives and move forward to a new winning plan.

Cycle

Winners stop the losers cycle or habits and plan to win. They stop blaming others. They concentrate on healing their wound from deep and move on to a brighter future.

Skills

Winners learn new skills to lead their way in life successfully.

The action starts within you

You have to decide that you need to change. A change for a better future and for having it all.

Create your future by clear and positive imagination

Think of what you really want to have in life. Set realistic goals, create a clear idea, and stick to it every day.

Review your goals and focus on them often, in mind, in writing, and in action.

Keep in mind, positive thinking, positive energy, and positive imagination.

When you feel a negative force, deal with it in a positive way and take advantage of the learning experience. Use the experience to get closer to your dream life.

Find total peace. Relax and let go. You need to find peace of mind. Stop struggling, stop trying so hard, stop doing so much, and give yourself a total break for a while. Then you can concentrate all your energy on what is truly important to you on the road to achieving your goals and dreams.

Make a connection with your inner self. You need to make the right connection with your inner self to be able to make positive changes in your life. Living for here and now, inner peace, open mind, free spirit, positive attitude, relaxed, and seeing every adventure as a learning process rather than an obstacle.

Condition your intention in creating your future. Be true to your dreams. Be honest to yourself. Is this what you really desire to see and to have? In case of hesitation and doubts think twice, because this is a good indication that this may not be your true goal.

It is in your mind

The answer to my friend's question is "never quit". You are made to be a believer. Humans are made to be creators.

Create what you want to see in your mind and adopt it by the heart.

Believe in your dreams, and they will lead your future. Don't let anyone to tell you this is not possible. Don't let anyone to rule your life.

Take an inventory of yourself.

Start with deep soul searching.

You have to be honest with your feelings. Express your ideas clearly to others. Don't expect others to read your mind. You cannot expect others to help you with your dream life if you don't face the reality of your dreams and express clearly what you want.

If you are looking to find friends then be a friend first. If you are searching for a true partner to share your life with then be honest to others and say what you are looking for without hesitations. If having a better job is in your mind then set your goals to get it. Get real with your thoughts and work at it to turn your dreams into reality.

Do you love yourself?
Describe all your beauties and your qualities:

_____

_____

_____

_____

_____

_____

How do you rate your character?

_____

_____

_____

_____

_____

_____

How do you see the child in you?

_____

_____

_____

_____

_____

_____

What kind of mental attitude do you carry?

_____

_____

_____

_____

_____

_____

_____

How do you fight your battles?

_____

_____

_____

_____

_____

_____

What do you do in times of difficulties?

_____

_____

_____

_____

_____

_____

Chapter 3—The Battle

The battle of life is to find a place where we feel happy and fulfilled. This knowledge makes the decision to achieve our dreams very easy. This way we know what we really want to be in life. We know to love ourselves unselfishly and fight for our happiness.

The fight for your dream life does not mean you need to put others down in the process. It simply means to discover your true call and fight for it. If you don't fight for your happiness, who will?

You are the only one who can think for you. You've got to do it for you.

What the mind can believe can be achieved in life. Regardless of who you are or what you have been, you can be what you want to be.

Where is your passion?

Find your true passion in life.

Passion can be found anywhere that opens up enthusiasm in you.

Passion is where a voice deep inside you says there is more to it. Something more is out there and I am going to make it happen.

What is your dream?

_____

_____

_____

_____

_____

_____

What is your passion in life?

_____

_____

_____

_____

_____

_____

Have the desire to be more. See the possibilities for the future.

Direct your thoughts, and be excited to create a better future.

Be Real

Take control of your emotions and lead a positive action. Being real means that you need to face your life clearly to be able to deal with it toward achieving a better life. You can do this by being positive to yourself. By changing the negative thoughts that is been given to you and replacing them by positives. Now you can be the master of your life.

Is this my road? Is this the road I want to be in? Is this road going to lead my dream life?

_____

_____

_____

_____

_____

_____

_____

Who is responsible for my decision-making?

_____

_____

_____

_____

_____

_____

_____

What if failure happens? How would I respond to failure?

_____

_____

_____

_____

_____

_____

What can I do when failure happens? What is my plan of action to get positive results out of failure?

_____

_____

_____

_____

_____

_____

Are you afraid of success? What do you think happens if you become successful? What is my plan of action to stay focused with my dream life in time of success. Write down every thing that you are afraid of:

_____

_____

_____

_____

_____

_____

The right mental attitude

Get all the positive forces on your side.

Having faith
This means you are willing to take risks, you know there is something bigger and better out there that you are going to reach for it and get to your destination.

Hope
Hope is an ultimate super power spirit lifter. Having hope will give you the vision for a better future and it fights against the obstacles coming your way. Never let hope out of your site.

Being optimistic
This is a good skill to keep the positive energy around. It will show you all the possibilities out there. Your optimistic vision will lead you to stand up to any hardship.

Have integrity
Your courage is a great asset that fully empowers you.

Be passionate
See the heart in whatever you encounter, be generous, and kind.

Tolerance
See and hear things clearly as they are. See the differences in people, places, and thing's, and respect them all.

Good common sense
This is a tool to keep you in balance for making the right decisions.

New Era

There will always be obstacles and difficult challenges in all stages of life. The only way to have your dream life is to see the obstacles clearly and to be able to resolve them into your advantage.

When an obstacle shows it's face, look into the message hidden in the challenge. Always question the obstacle. Is it your weakness, your lack of knowledge in that particular area, or simply a message to make you better and stronger in life?

Life will always be full of challenges. The good news is that we are in a new era. The new era brings understanding and accessibility. The new era offers great knowledge available to everyone. There is nothing you can't find. There is nothing you can't defeat. All you have to do is ask.

Your mission is to keep a positive attitude at all times. Having a positive attitude won't keep you away from the obstacles in life, but it will help you conquer the challenges and help you move forward.

Have no tolerance for potential killers

The most dangerous potential killer on the road to achieve your dream life is *negative thoughts.*

Any negativity that enters your mind has the potential to destroy your dream.

Yes, negative thoughts are extremely dangerous. Do not allow negativity to enter your mind either through yourself or by others.

The real negatives are the ones that will keep you from moving forward toward your goals in life.

Some examples of negativity would be "this is not possible", "I can't make it," or "you are not worthy."

Negative thoughts are forbidden to enter the mind of a successful happy person.

People who want to achieve the best in life only allow positive thoughts to enter their minds.

Turn your obstacles into opportunities.

Keep in mind that not all problems are considered as negative!

When a problem shows its face, don't look at it as a negative matter. Look at the situation carefully and ask yourself what lies behind it, and try to fix it.

When someone complains about something, try to find a solution.

When a maverick shows a different point of view or disagrees with you, listen.

These issues won't be considered as negatives, but as opportunities to make things better.

Successful people take criticism as a leading road to a powerful future.

Find the messages in anything coming your way and make it better.

Build your morale to its highest level.

Be sure of yourself

Build your self-confidence by being proud of yourself. The way you can be proud of yourself is by knowing who you really are.

Know yourself

Be proud of yourself the way you are. Don't judge yourself if you have been judged wrong. Try to keep your energy up and work on the unwanted situation to make things better for your life.

Be positive

Always keep a positive attitude to be able to achieve your highest dreams.

Be direct

No one is a mind reader. Don't assume anything. Just tell it like it is. If you want people to know what you want, you have to tell them what you have in mind with respect. You have to direct people, and the best way is direct communication.

Leave nothing to chance

Plan and follow through with every aspect of your life.

Take control, lead your life.

I am worthy. I can do it. I am the one. I'll make it happen.

Be your own messenger

Get real with life. Dare to imagine your highest dreams.

What is going to hold you back? What are you afraid of? Remember, nothing can hold you back. Nothing at all.

When the calling is within your heart, nothing will hold you back from reaching your goals.

Reinforce what you are trying to accomplish every day of your life.

Send clear messages to yourself and others.

Set-up and review your goals clearly.

Don't let others do your job.

Get advice from experts, the ones who have taken the road.

Take action.

Taking any little step toward a goal will capture maximum accomplishments in a long run.

True change always comes with some sense of discomfort

We are all jugglers in life. We keep a balance with our careers, home, children, family, relationships, friends, chores, financial matters, and more.

There will always be some sort of discomfort in any taken areas of our lives. If you sense a need to change for better, do it.

There will be normal changes, and some not normal, in all areas, ages, or stages of life.

The normal and constant changes are like growing up, starting school, getting to know and adjust with our new environment, relationships, marriage, divorce, moving to a new city, fighting a sickness, tragedies, and so on.

Any change in life, whether normal or out of ordinary, will bring stress. The best power you can have is to get equipped with the knowledge to comfort yourself and handle the situation in the best possible way.

Accept the changes and use your resources to move forward with your life.

Turn a disadvantage into an advantage.

Fear

What is holding you back from living your dream life?

Fear is normal as long as you realize it and find a way to overcome it.

It is time to find solutions if fear is keeping you away from experiencing life.

Always keep in mind that there is a way out no matter what happens. You can handle the situation by finding the best resources to fight back.

The nature of your fear

People are afraid of changes, darkness, aging, dying, rejection, success, and the unknown.

These days people are afraid of the world as they know ending; the crime on the streets and in their homes; inflation; medical bills; aging; marriage; divorce; commitment; caffeine, sugar, salt; failure; success; and many more.

What are your fears?

_____

_____

_____

_____

_____

_____

_____

_____

_____

_____

_____

_____

_____

_____

_____

_____

_____

_____

_____

_____

_____

_____

_____

_____

_____

Fear of Change

We go through many minor and major changes in different stages of our life. Accept that nothing stays the same. Realize that change happens. Get equipped with the right knowledge and how you can cope with difficulties.

Negative Programming

A mom sends her child to school, kisses the child goodbye and says, "be careful out there". The child learns there must be something out there that they need to be careful of. What is it, How do I know how to cope with it? Negative programming, regardless of how light or severe, is a major cause of fear.

Action Oriented Fear

Ending or beginning a relationship, being assertive, going on an interview, making friends.

Ego Oriented Fear

Loss of ones' image, rejection, success, the feeling of helplessness, disapproval, being conned, making a mistake, just to name a few.

The Magic Solution against Fear

> ➢ Trust yourself more, trust God.
> ➢ Be resourceful and knowledgeable.
> ➢ The more information you get, the better you can handle any situation.
> ➢ Just do it. Take one step at a time.
> ➢ The joy of discovery is delicious.
> ➢ Trust your ability.
> ➢ Train yourself by constantly saying: "I know the ways to take care of it."
> ➢ Sharpen your power vocabulary to all positive thinking.
> ➢ Nod your head "yes," start your thinking process with accepting not denying.
> ➢ Agreement gives you the sense that everything will be all right because you are going to make it all right.
> ➢ Breathe deep and relax your body, let the tension go.
> ➢ Look for value in any given situation.
> ➢ Don't push difficulties aside. Say yes and find ways to handle any situations.

Commit yourself to pushing through the fear and becoming more than what you are at the present moment. You just need to welcome everything that comes into your life in any matter or form.

Learn the power and energy of your higher self.

If you need to know more about fear I recommend this book: *"Feel the fear and do it anyway."* by: Susan Jeffers, Ph.D.* She talks about different types of fears and how to overcome them. She ends her book this way.

"As you live the life to the fullest, by welcoming everything that lies in the power of learning to get to the higher self, moment by moment, day by day, in perfect time, you will find yourself moving closer and closer to home. The paradox is that when you stay close to home, you can go anywhere and do anything without fear. The divine Homesickness disappears as you find the place where we all are connected as loving human beings."

Still have anxiety and fear?

Get busy with life.

Try to get involved with your community do volunteer work.

Get plenty of rest. Cut down on sugar and caffeine, and exercise.

Help others. The ultimate happiness is the ability to help others.

---

*   *"Feel the fear and do it anyway"*—This book is available for purchase on DesignYourDreamLife.com

Inner Strength

Our instinct is our radar. But we tend to ignore it. The more we ignore it; the farther behind it will leave us.

We need to learn to look at our inner instincts, listen to them and follow the right direction.

By recognizing what you truly want you will be able to find the balance in all that concerns you. The right balance that is needed to keep you on the road. The road you need to achieve the highest in relationships, love, health, happiness, and success in all that you desire and matters.

Chapter 4—Three Golden Rules

1. Appreciate what you have.
— Come to peace with your childhood experience.

— Come to peace with past obstacles.

— Accept all your experiences as a token of getting enriched in life.

— Come to peace with you and your life.

2. Know what is next.
— No matter which road you take, obstacles are here to stay.

— Come to peace with obstacles and learn to handle them to your advantage.

— Pamper yourself, nourish your body, motivate your brain, and challenge your knowledge.

3. Design your dream life.
— Always be aware of your surrounding. Look, listen, breath well, enjoy the nature.

— Learn the art of observation, listening, and learning. No matter where you are and what you do.

— Plan your life starting with your dreams and never rest until you get what you want.

Old Chinese saying:

"No one is your friend. No one is your enemy. But everyone is your teacher."

We are here to learn, learn, and learn more.

And to pass it onto others.

Grief

Life is full of changes, full of problems, and the never-ending challenges. When you know that life is full of surprises, it won't be a surprise anymore. You will look to it clearly, you'll expect it, and you will get equipped to confront it. Learn the experience and grow with it.

You have a pain; you have lost a love, a love that is not here any longer. Remind yourself, that love is not lost. It is not here, but is always close to you.

Recognize your grieve. Give yourself time to grieve, cry, talk, think, and go through the process. It is normal.

Allow a little happiness in your life. Do it slowly if you like, but do it. Your loved ones want to see you well.

Discuss your feelings. Find a support group. Talk to people.

— Go for a long walk.
— Drink plenty of liquids.
— Take your vitamins and eat right.

Have the courage to grieve, then let go

When your skin burns it takes a long time to heal. It is the same when your soul gets hurt. But you must know how to come to peace with your hurt feelings to heal your soul. You need to accept and express your feelings. Talk about the things that are bothering you. If you have lost a loved one then talk about the good times you had together. Keep their memories alive with you. Go to the process of grief then release your energy to get your life back together.

Look into other opportunities in front of you.

Explore beyond your limits, Accept new challenges and learn.

Do volunteer work to help other people.

Shift your thoughts toward the positive.

Move on to the next stage of our life. The circle of life needs you and what you have to offer.

Developing a Healing Mind

When faced with disease or disability, we have a choice. We can choose to become discouraged and invite defeat and depression. Or we can choose life.

How do we choose life?

Focus on the wonderful, mighty and beautiful things around you. This will help you from falling into the pit of self-pity that's always beckoning when a challenge has its black grip on you.

Focus on purpose. We are here for a purpose. Each of us has a role to fulfill in life. Finding joy and pursuing the unique tasks and challenges that lie before us.

Focus on sharing peace and joy.

Focus on positive action.

Focus on forgiving. You can't harbor resentment or bury hurt. You must throw them away.

Focus on acceptance. The world might not seem perfect and we have not been perfect in it. But, God's love is unconditional. Everything has it's own purpose.

Focus on others. Numerous studies show that regular, positive social interaction tends to enhance our overall well-being and limit depressive episodes.

Focus on fellowship. Studies have also shown, people who follow their fellowship regularly, tend to get sick less often, heal quicker, and live longer.

Free yourself

Leave nothing to chance.

No bondage

Don't let obstacles keep you from reaching the best you can be in life.

External influences

There will be many challenges on your road to design your dream life. But, no one says it will be spring every day of your life. No one said that winter is not beautiful. There will be times when you have to protect yourself from thunder. Be prepared to protect yourself against the negative external influences and enjoy the rest.

Internal negative influences

Are there any negative influences in your life from past or present? Toss them out. You don't have to hide them. Confront them, find help, overcome and bring peace back into your life.

Always do what you want to do

Have the courage to say no, to stand up for your thoughts and not let anyone walk over them.

Your taste is for sure different than your parents, friends, or anyone else. Be proud of yourself and stick to your ideas.

Face the truth

Do the right thing when it comes to making decisions.

Chapter 5—Thriving on Risk

Christopher Columbus took the chance to sail the oceans because he believed there was something better out there. He believed in his dream to achieve more. He took the chance, fought the obstacles, and lived an adventurous life.

He planned it. He lived it. And he enjoyed living it.

Are you willing to take risks in achieving your dream life?

Focus
Break the old habits and bring in new ones.

Life challenges
Stay on track in times of trouble, or when obstacles stand in the way,

Flexibility
Bend but don't break. Eliminate non-essentials and take care of priorities. This should be in your everyday success plan.

Achievement
If you want something, go after it, ask for it, and fight for it.

Getting help
Ask for advice from someone who can help. The one with experience, the one who can say I have done it, the one who can show you the road.

Areas of weakness

There will be frustration, one struggle after another, problems, and many obstacles in searching for your dream life.

Personal inventory

The winning plan to achieve your dream life is to be able to balance all areas in your lifestyle.

List the areas that are lacking your attention?

_____

_____

_____

_____

_____

_____

_____

_____

_____

_____

_____

_____

_____

_____

_____

_____

Which areas need more strength?

_____

_____

_____

_____

_____

_____

_____

_____

_____

_____

_____

What are the obstacles?

_____

_____

_____

_____

_____

_____

_____

_____

_____

_____

_____

Write your action plan on how to achieve a balance in all areas of your life.

_____

_____

_____

_____

_____

_____

_____

_____

_____

_____

_____

_____

_____

_____

_____

_____

Schedule the winning plan

Environment

We are subject to our environment; therefore you need to select your surroundings to serve your purpose in order to meet your desired objective.

Uninterrupted time frames

Make sure you control your environment. Set your daily schedule to make the most of your day and give it your full attention. Turn off the TV, the phone, and anything else that might take your attention away from reaching your daily assignments. Avoid situations, associations, or acquaintances that hold you back from your desired goal.

Prepare for interruptions

You might get some interruptions no matter how well you establish your schedule. Therefore, be prepared to adjust accordingly. Occasional interruptions are okay, accept it, and give your attention to the situation that needs your attention. You can go back to your regular schedule after you resolve them.

Productivity times

Work smarter, not harder. Think about the stages, right task, right time, and attention ahead of time.

Prioritize

No matter how high your energy level is, we get tired and need rest. Do priority matters during your high energy level hours, and spread the other chores to when your energy level is lower.

Direction

Your sense of control is to know where you are going and how you are going to accomplish this. Stay on course and follow your plans.

Time

There is always a limited amount of time in hours and days. Use it to your advantage.

Deadlines

Do the right job. Keep in mind that quality is worth more than quantity. Always calculate a little bit more delay on the actual deadlines.

Readjustments

If your plans are not going the way they should, regroup, try again, and look at different angles.

Be selective

Successful people are selective about their choices in life. Every issue matters and needs a special attention.

Arm yourself to resist temptations

Count your blessings. Keep a healthy mind in times of challenges and focus on your better personality.

Happiness

Take pleasure in your daily life. Reward your challenges. Enjoy your achievements no matter how small and give yourself a pat on the back. Have a sense of humor. Watch more comedy shows. Laugh and smile a lot.

Being Resourceful

Learning takes time, sometimes years of practicing, experiencing, and polishing. Learn to climb up the mountain, one step at a time.

Learning occurs when you stay with the process from the beginning to the finish. Learning occurs by doing.

Research

Learn from mentors and search for more guidance. Review successful behaviors and reshape your own practices.

Training

Develop new skills to improve your chances for success.

Nourish your curiosity

Learn like a child, always eager to do, be open to new ideas, and say yes.

Explore

Expand your horizons and learn new things.

Keep learning

Learn to accept new ideas, learn from criticism, and stay on top of learning more.

Acquiring Skills

The successful system is to find the genius in you. All you need to do is to find the skills of the trade. Success just doesn't happen. You make success happen by applying your skills.

Thinking skills

Generate alternatives to find the best result in any given situations.

Personality skills

Learn the skills to manage your life in the best possible way, to recognize your weaknesses, and your strengths, and to empower your life.

Training skills

Learn the facts, know the meaning, use the power, exercise the power, work out solutions, and be resourceful.

Adaptability skills

It is how to adapt yourself satisfactory to your environment. Do you adjust well to places, persons, situations, and things?

Know-how activities

Do you observe situations the way they are or by your own point of view? Do you practice attentive listening? Do you know how to solve problems when needed?

Do you adjust well to new places, people, situations, and unfamiliar things?

_____

_____

_____

_____

_____

Do you observe situations the way they are or with your own point of view?

_____

_____

_____

_____

_____

Do you practice attentive listening?

_____

_____

_____

_____

_____

Do you know how to solve problems when needed?

_____

_____

_____

_____

_____

Get Enough Rest

The ultimate challenge for you is to keep balance in all you have and in all matters of your life.

Trying to keep the perfect balance in body, spirit and mind means that you need to take a good care of yourself.

Healthy diet
Keep balanced, varied, healthy eating habits in your lifestyle.

Active
Be active and keep a good balance of physical activities in your life.

Balance
Maintain balance in all matters of your life.

Relax
Set aside a time for relaxation, meditation, renewing your thoughts, and restoring your energy.

Goals for a Greater Good

What are the true riches in life?

_____

_____

_____

_____

_____

_____

_____

_____

What do true riches mean to you?

_____

_____

_____

_____

_____

_____

_____

- Discover new possibilities
- New challenges
- Seek true meaning of riches in life for you
- Change your lifestyle to a winning format
- Improve the overall quality of human life

Money

Money plays an important role in our life. Is money ruling your life, or you?

What is the role of money in your life?

_____

_____

_____

_____

_____

_____

Do you think you have enough to satisfy your lifestyle?

_____

_____

_____

_____

_____

_____

What are your plans to have enough money to satisfy your lifestyle?

_____

_____

_____

_____

_____

_____

How to Handle Your Treasure

There are stories of rich men who lost it all and those who made mil-
lions from nothing. Having or not having enough money should be
the least of your worries, if you know how to handle it right. So, what
is the secret?

Having it all in terms of money is not so much in having more money.
It is knowing how to manage the money no matter how much you
have.

To make more money you need to use your mind, skills, resources,
energy, brain, and more. However, the most important thing is to manage your money the best possible way to bring you more money.

Wealth means managing all aspects of your life in a perfectly balanced
way and money is part of it.

The first step is to focus on your standard of living, the way you want
to live, rather than money.

Focus on the style of your choice. Change your surroundings the way
you feel comfortable with and the way it is a reflection of you.

Learn the basic rules of managing money. This will show you where to
start and then expand on it to where you want to be.

Basic rules of money management

Watch how you are spending your cash

For every $10 you put in your wallet, take off nine. Forget about the extra dollar, you will be amaze at how fast it grows into a sizable saving.

Controlling expenditures

Write down the important things you need and select only what you must have. Make wise investments.

Make the gold multiply

Use the stock market, buy government bonds, and guard your treasures from loss.

Invest

Invest only where the principal is safe, where it can be reclaimed when desired, and where you will not fail to collect a fair interest. Consult those who have successfully done the job.

Make the dwelling a profitable investment

Get rid of debt. Get rid of credit card debts and use credit cards only when necessary and pay on time. Own your home.

Charity

Money you give will come back to you two folds. Give money to charities that you believe in.

Save

Start your savings plan by simply putting away your change. Save any change you get back from daily cash spending. Put it away. Count it after a year and use it to open a savings account. This is a pleasant habit that won't change your lifestyle a bit.

Save by getting rid of clutter

It is easy to get tempted in this life by beautiful things. However, you only need to know it is not what you see, but what you really need to manage your life better. When you are completely satisfied with the management and savings, then you can spend on luxuries.

Save by not buying cheap and low quality stuff only for the mere fact that they are cheap. If you don't need it, don't buy it. Ask yourself, should I buy this product, or should I put this money in my savings. Then you will have made the right decision by not paying for junk.

Save by living simple but elegant. If it is not a necessity don't buy it. If you are not using it, sell it.

No guilty feelings

If you get an uncomfortable feeling in your stomach when you purchase something, then return it right away and put the money in your savings account. Whenever you get a guilty feeling, it means that is not right for you at this time.

Manage your daily snacks

Drink water instead of soda. Take vegetables and crackers to work. Avoid the snack machines. Put the money you save in your change account or savings account.

Don't pay for friends

Don't pay for friends merely for getting their approvals or attention. Go Dutch when going out to lunch or dinner. If it is your treat, invite them to your house and cook a pleasant meal. Take what you save by treating your friends at home and put it in your savings account.

Open a savings account

Save, save, save. You have to save no matter what. Open a savings account and save as little as 25 dollars a month regardless of how much debt you have or how far behind you get on your loan payments.

Set budgets

Set your budget by separating "fixed" monthly payments like your home mortgage and car loan payment, and "variable" payments like birthday gifts and entertainment.

Refinance your home for a lower monthly mortgage payment. [Visit Finance on www.DesignYourDreamLife.com]

What is your long-term plan? You need to set specific goals to pay off debts, Savings for retirement, children's collage, pension plans, and make a commitment to make it happen.

Spending habits

Watch carefully where your cash goes. Remember you are wasting your money if you are spending it on things that are not necessary to have.

Save, save, save. You need to pay yourself first even if you are in debt. Invest the money that you have saved, let your money make money for you, and then pay your debts.

Organize and set plans for every issue in its place. Budget plan for "fixed" payments; "fluctuate" payments, savings, pay off debts, investments, charity, and more.

Keep tap on your spending. Keep track of your spending by binning them in specific categories such as Birthday parties, gifts, lunch treats, movie tickets, and so on. Set aside a small notebook to jot down daily cash spending.

Make your budget work for you by making smart spending decisions. Leave room for the stuff that makes you happy.

Management

It is time to clean up your act and keep up with your dream life. Having it all need work and commitment.

You need to feel the strength in your heart, see yourself the way you want to, and capture the power within your grasp.

Having the ability to manage all aspects of your life, personally, socially, physically, and emotionally.

Lay the proper foundation to be able to keep track and identify measurable steps.

Time management

Set specific schedules for your chores. Learn how to zero in by blocking out distractions.

Setting priorities

Use your high-energy hours when things need more attention. Look at your daily activity list and see what you can most efficiently accomplish.

People management

Surround yourself with positive people, help the ones who need help, and get help from the ones who have the knowledge and ability to help you.

Environment management

We are part of our environment. Set your surroundings so it will fit the best way for achieving your goals. Your environment has to serve you. When you feel good about your environment then you will feel good about yourself.

Money management

Keep track of your spending, budgeting, investments, credit control, saving, and money-making strategies. Let your money work for you by using your mind, talent, skills, and management.

Keep things organized

Being organized at home, school, and work means being prepared. And being prepared will give you more time and energy to spend toward reaching your goals.

Balance

The key to success is keeping a balance in everything you do. Manage your time, money, family, career, and give everything a chance to have the right balance of your attention.

Chapter 6—Action Plan

What specific things can you do?

You are a smart, nice, people person, you have so many talents, but where do you start? How do you go about changing your dream and making it into reality?

You need to draw a map from the start to finish.

Plan your action program and win the tasks by doing it.

— Make your statement.
— Get rid of procrastination.
— No buts, no anxiety.
— Work smarter, not harder.
— When you set out to do something, don't come back until you have it done.
— Plan your days and your thoughts.

This is how I see my future and myself:

_____

_____

_____

_____

_____

_____

_____

_____

_____

_____

Where do I see procrastination?

_____

_____

_____

_____

_____

_____

_____

_____

_____

_____

_____

_____

My plans to rid myself of procrastination:

_____

_____

_____

_____

_____

_____

_____

_____

_____

_____

_____

_____

Do I have any anxiety toward achieving my dream life?

_____

_____

_____

_____

_____

_____

_____

_____

_____

_____

_____

_____

My plans to handle my anxiety:

_____

_____

_____

_____

_____

_____

_____

_____

_____

_____

_____

These are my goals to achieve in life:

_____

_____

_____

_____

_____

_____

_____

_____

_____

_____

_____

This is my plan to achieve my goals:

_____

_____

_____

_____

_____

_____

_____

_____

_____

_____

_____

_____

_____

_____

_____

_____

_____

_____

_____

_____

_____

_____

_____

_____

_____

_____

Guidance Journal

You need to set specific rules to guide your way.

For example, you say, "I love to jog". Just saying it won't make it happen, unless you set specific plans for it. Ask yourself where to jog, for how long, what time of the day, and follow through.

Being specific in setting your goals is a great asset to have.

- Set specific goals
- Project what you are going to make happen
- Build your success plan
- Plan in detail

This is a method to let you win your life again and again. This is a workbook for you to review things from inside and out.

You need to work on these matters throughout your life. Make this book a journal to lead your dream life. All you need to do is to fill in the blanks and turn your thoughts into actions.

Set Yourself Free

Your reality comes from your mind.

Your thoughts start with dreams.

Your dreams will become your reality by believing in the possibilities.

You become what you dream.

Why aren't you getting the things you want or being where you want to be?

Discover what is holding you back and set yourself free.

What is holding you back?

Is perfectionism holding you back?

Do you expect everything to be perfect? Is your expectation of perfectionism holding you back? Do you not do things unless everything is perfect? Write down your thoughts:

_____

_____

_____

_____

_____

_____

_____

_____

_____

_____

_____

_____

_____

_____

_____

_____

_____

_____

_____

Do you procrastinate as a dreamer?
Are you a dreamer, not a doer? Do you procrastinate in this matter?

_____

_____

_____

_____

_____

_____

_____

_____

_____

_____

_____

Do you worry a lot? **List the things that worry you.**

_____

_____

_____

_____

_____

_____

_____

_____

_____

_____

Are you afraid of challenges that future might bring?
Do you think about unknown future or circumstances?

_____

_____

_____

_____

_____

_____

_____

_____

_____

_____

_____

_____

_____

_____

_____

_____

_____

_____

_____

_____

_____

_____

Daily chores

Do small tasks hold you back from getting the big picture? List all your daily tasks

_____

_____

_____

_____

_____

_____

_____

_____

_____

_____

_____

_____

_____

_____

_____

_____

_____

_____

_____

_____

_____

Do you delay your chores?

Do you leave everything for the last minute? Write down the things you usually leave till the last minute.

_____

_____

_____

_____

_____

_____

_____

_____

_____

_____

_____

_____

_____

_____

_____

_____

_____

_____

_____

_____

_____

_____

_____

Do you feel there is too much to do? Explain:

_____

_____

_____

_____

_____

_____

_____

_____

_____

_____

_____

What makes you feel free?

_____

_____

_____

_____

_____

_____

_____

_____

_____

_____

_____

What makes you feel beautiful?

_____

_____

_____

_____

_____

_____

_____

_____

_____

_____

_____

_____

_____

_____

_____

_____

_____

_____

_____

_____

_____

_____

_____

DARE TO WIN

Awaken your dream life.

What am I waiting for?

_____

_____

_____

_____

_____

_____

_____

_____

_____

_____

_____

_____

_____

_____

_____

_____

_____

_____

_____

_____

_____

What would you like to be?

_____

_____

_____

_____

_____

_____

_____

_____

_____

_____

_____

_____

_____

_____

_____

_____

_____

_____

_____

_____

_____

_____

_____

_____

_____

What would you like to have?

_____

_____

_____

_____

_____

_____

_____

_____

_____

_____

_____

_____

_____

_____

_____

_____

_____

_____

_____

_____

_____

_____

_____

_____

What is your true passion in life?

_____

_____

_____

_____

_____

_____

_____

_____

_____

_____

_____

_____

_____

_____

_____

_____

_____

_____

_____

_____

_____

_____

_____

What are your talents?

_____

_____

_____

_____

_____

_____

_____

_____

_____

_____

_____

_____

_____

_____

_____

_____

_____

_____

_____

_____

_____

_____

_____

_____

_____

What are your hobbies?

_____

_____

_____

_____

_____

_____

_____

_____

_____

_____

_____

_____

_____

_____

_____

_____

_____

_____

_____

_____

_____

_____

_____

Do you dare to take risks?

_____

_____

_____

_____

_____

_____

_____

_____

_____

_____

_____

If you could do whatever you wanted to, what would it be?

_____

_____

_____

_____

_____

_____

_____

_____

_____

_____

_____

What are your greatest strengths?

_____

_____

_____

_____

_____

_____

_____

_____

_____

_____

_____

_____

_____

_____

_____

_____

_____

_____

_____

_____

_____

_____

_____

_____

With whom do you like to associate?

_____

_____

_____

_____

_____

_____

_____

_____

_____

_____

What trades do you know?

_____

_____

_____

_____

_____

_____

_____

_____

_____

_____

What trades would you like to explore?

_____

_____

_____

_____

_____

_____

_____

_____

_____

_____

_____

_____

_____

_____

_____

_____

_____

_____

_____

_____

_____

_____

_____

_____

_____

_____

What are your great ideas?

_____

_____

_____

_____

_____

_____

_____

_____

_____

_____

_____

_____

_____

_____

_____

_____

_____

_____

_____

_____

_____

_____

_____

GOAL ANALYSIS

Whose mind do you lean on?

_____

_____

_____

_____

_____

_____

_____

_____

_____

What does your mind tell you?

_____

_____

_____

_____

_____

_____

_____

_____

_____

How are you leading your life? What is it all about?

What are your goals?

_____

_____

_____

_____

_____

_____

_____

_____

_____

_____

_____

_____

_____

_____

_____

_____

_____

_____

_____

_____

_____

_____

_____

How are you planning to get where you want to be?

_____

_____

_____

_____

_____

_____

_____

_____

_____

_____

_____

_____

_____

_____

_____

_____

_____

_____

_____

_____

_____

_____

_____

_____

When is the time to plan your dream life?

_____

_____

_____

_____

_____

_____

_____

_____

_____

_____

Are you set to plan now for tomorrow?

_____

_____

_____

_____

_____

_____

_____

_____

_____

_____

How do you plan to get it done?

_____

_____

_____

_____

_____

_____

_____

_____

_____

_____

What are your plans to put your dream life together?

_____

_____

_____

_____

_____

_____

_____

_____

_____

_____

_____

What are your plans on organizing your home life?

_____

_____

_____

_____

_____

_____

_____

_____

_____

_____

_____

_____

_____

_____

_____

_____

_____

_____

_____

_____

_____

_____

_____

_____

What are your plans on organizing your career life?

_____

_____

_____

_____

_____

_____

_____

_____

_____

_____

_____

_____

_____

_____

_____

_____

_____

_____

_____

_____

_____

_____

_____

_____

_____

_____

_____

Chapter 7—The Power to Design Your Dream Life

This book is designed to lead you to your dream life.

Now you have to put them into actions and move beyond your potential.

The 30 "Power Rules" for setting your proper foundation

1. Purpose

2. Program

3. Position

4. Principles

5. Problems

6. Pain

7. Parents

8. Patience

9. Paper and pen

10. People

11. Persistence

12. Plan

13. Practice

14. Production

15. Publicity

16. Progress

17. Promotion

18. Profession

19. Passionate

20. Place

21. Penny

22. Partner

24. Pal

25. Patterns

26. Positive

27. Paradise

28. Peace

29. Prayer

30. Power of proper foundation

1. Purpose

To find the purpose is to look for the motivation.

What is your motivation?

Where is your determination?

How do you get inspired?

2. Program

Program your mind as a winner to lead you in a positive way.

3. Position

Position yourself in a winning matter, image, posture, and attitude.

4. Principles

Learn the rules, regulations, and skills to empower your insights.

5. Problems

Deal with them. Respond to the obstacles.

6. Pain

Deal with it, do your grieving, and go on to be a better and stronger you.

7. Parents

It is your life now. Direct it the way you want it to be.

8. Patience

Know the timing, when to stay put, and when its time to move.

9. Paper and pen

> Write everything down; use them as your friends.

10. People

> Find support, build a good team, and resources.

11. Persistence

> Keep going, follow through, stay focused, never quit, and be full of determination.

12. Plan

> Keep your agendas, make a blueprint of your plans and goals in all areas of your life.

13. Practice

> Humans learn by doing, training, practice, and creative visualization. Do it more.

14. Production

> Set plans for your immediate, intermediate, and long-term goals.

15. Publicity

> Let others know what your plans are. Ask the experts for help and let others help you.

16. Progress

> Set up a system to keep track of your progress.

17. *Promotion*

Don't get stuck in a level—reach higher, and explore other opportunities.

18. *Profession*

Choose what is closer to your heart. Ask an expert in times of need.

19. *Passionate*

Be passionate in life, going to the heart of the matters

20. *Place*

Make your environment cater to your needs.

21. *Penny*

Organizing your financial matters and manage your money to work for you.

22. *Partner*

Give more, expect respect, listen, and be each other's friends.

24. *Pal*

Your pal is a great asset in times of good and bad.

25. *Patterns*

Tune yourself like a piano. Old habits die hard. Get rid of habits that are working against you. Discipline your schedule toward positive reinforcement.

26. *Positive*

Be positive and don't let any negative thoughts take hold of you.

27. *Paradise*

Your paradise is in your eyes.

28. *Peace*

Make peace with yourself.

29. *Prayer*

The greatest power a man posses, is the power of prayer.

30. *Power*

Build a proper foundation

The ultimate success

is

in your hands.

Fill in your personal thoughts and action plans.

What are you committed to?

_____

_____

_____

_____

_____

_____

_____

_____

_____

_____

_____

_____

_____

_____

_____

_____

_____

_____

_____

_____

_____

_____

What are you out for?

_____

_____

_____

_____

_____

_____

_____

_____

_____

_____

_____

_____

_____

_____

_____

_____

_____

_____

_____

_____

_____

_____

_____

_____

_____

What do you love?

_____

_____

_____

_____

_____

_____

_____

_____

_____

_____

_____

_____

_____

_____

_____

_____

_____

_____

_____

_____

_____

_____

_____

What are you committed to see happening in the world and in your life?

_____

_____

_____

_____

_____

_____

_____

_____

_____

_____

_____

_____

_____

_____

_____

_____

_____

_____

_____

_____

_____

_____

_____

_____

_____

What is your heart's desire?

_____

_____

_____

_____

_____

_____

_____

_____

_____

_____

_____

_____

_____

_____

_____

_____

_____

_____

_____

_____

_____

_____

_____

What is it for?

_____
_____
_____
_____
_____
_____
_____
_____
_____
_____
_____
_____
_____
_____
_____
_____
_____
_____
_____
_____
_____
_____
_____
_____
_____

What would that allow for?

_____

_____

_____

_____

_____

_____

_____

_____

_____

_____

_____

_____

_____

_____

_____

_____

_____

_____

_____

_____

_____

_____

_____

_____

How do you see yourself being the joyous person you meant to be?

_____

_____

_____

_____

_____

_____

_____

_____

_____

_____

_____

_____

_____

_____

_____

_____

_____

_____

_____

_____

_____

_____

_____

Close your eyes and imagine it has already happened. Write down whatever you imagined.

_____

_____

_____

_____

_____

_____

_____

_____

_____

_____

_____

_____

_____

_____

_____

_____

_____

_____

_____

_____

_____

_____

_____

Write down all of your commitments:

_____

_____

_____

_____

_____

_____

_____

_____

_____

_____

_____

_____

_____

_____

_____

_____

_____

_____

_____

_____

_____

_____

_____

_____

_____

_____

What are the obstacles that might get in your way?

_____

_____

_____

_____

_____

_____

_____

_____

_____

_____

_____

_____

_____

_____

_____

_____

_____

_____

_____

_____

_____

_____

_____

_____

Write down your ideas for possible solutions.

_____

_____

_____

_____

_____

_____

_____

_____

_____

_____

_____

_____

_____

_____

_____

_____

_____

_____

_____

_____

_____

_____

_____

_____

_____

What do you think could get in the way of accomplishing your goals?

_____

_____

_____

_____

_____

_____

_____

_____

_____

_____

_____

_____

_____

_____

_____

_____

_____

_____

_____

_____

_____

_____

_____

Chapter 8—Completion

Start with the things you want.

State your "I want" statements:

_____

_____

_____

_____

_____

_____

_____

_____

_____

_____

_____

_____

_____

_____

_____

_____

_____

_____

_____

_____

Things I want to change that I am not changing:

_____

_____

_____

_____

_____

_____

_____

_____

_____

_____

_____

_____

_____

_____

_____

_____

_____

_____

_____

_____

_____

_____

_____

_____

Things I want to stop:

_____

_____

_____

_____

_____

_____

_____

_____

_____

_____

_____

_____

_____

_____

_____

_____

_____

_____

_____

_____

_____

_____

_____

_____

_____

Things I started and want to finish:

_____

_____

_____

_____

_____

_____

_____

_____

_____

_____

_____

_____

_____

_____

_____

_____

_____

_____

_____

_____

_____

_____

_____

_____

Things I want to have and don't have:

_____

_____

_____

_____

_____

_____

_____

_____

_____

_____

_____

_____

_____

_____

_____

_____

_____

_____

_____

_____

_____

_____

_____

Things I want to do and never have done:

_____

_____

_____

_____

_____

_____

_____

_____

_____

_____

_____

_____

_____

_____

_____

_____

_____

_____

_____

_____

_____

_____

_____

_____

_____

Things I want to be and never have been:

Things I want to say and have not said:

_____

_____

_____

_____

_____

_____

_____

_____

_____

_____

_____

_____

_____

_____

_____

_____

_____

_____

_____

_____

_____

_____

_____

Anger I've had and have not expressed:

_____

_____

_____

_____

_____

_____

_____

_____

_____

_____

_____

_____

_____

_____

_____

_____

_____

_____

_____

_____

_____

_____

_____

_____

_____

Things I want to learn and never have learned:

_____

_____

_____

_____

_____

_____

_____

_____

_____

_____

_____

_____

_____

_____

_____

_____

_____

_____

_____

_____

_____

_____

Costs vs. Benefits
What are the benefits of staying the way I am?

_____

_____

_____

_____

_____

_____

_____

_____

_____

_____

_____

_____

_____

_____

_____

_____

_____

_____

_____

_____

_____

_____

_____

_____

_____

Reasons to stay in your box:

_____

_____

_____

_____

_____

_____

_____

_____

_____

_____

_____

_____

_____

_____

_____

_____

_____

_____

_____

_____

_____

_____

_____

_____

What is it costing me to continue to empower this paradigm?
Write down all the things you're losing out on:

_____

_____

_____

_____

_____

_____

_____

_____

_____

_____

_____

_____

_____

_____

_____

_____

_____

_____

_____

_____

_____

_____

_____

_____

What is it worth to you to change the future? Are you willing to let go of the old habits and redesign your life?

_____

_____

_____

_____

_____

_____

_____

_____

_____

_____

_____

_____

_____

_____

_____

_____

_____

_____

_____

_____

_____

_____

_____

Action

What is the pain in taking the action to change your life? What are the obstacles?

_____

_____

_____

_____

_____

_____

_____

_____

_____

_____

_____

_____

_____

_____

_____

_____

_____

_____

_____

_____

_____

_____

_____

_____

What are the rewards by taking the action?

_____

_____

_____

_____

_____

_____

_____

_____

_____

_____

_____

_____

_____

_____

_____

_____

_____

_____

_____

_____

_____

_____

_____

How do you get inspired to take actions?

_____

_____

_____

_____

_____

_____

_____

_____

_____

_____

_____

_____

_____

_____

_____

_____

_____

_____

_____

_____

_____

_____

_____

_____

What are your clear assignments to follow the action?

_____

_____

_____

_____

_____

_____

_____

_____

_____

_____

_____

_____

_____

_____

_____

_____

_____

_____

_____

_____

_____

_____

_____

What is your training and know-how to lead you to taking the action?

_____

_____

_____

_____

_____

_____

_____

_____

_____

_____

_____

_____

_____

_____

_____

_____

_____

_____

_____

_____

_____

_____

_____

_____

_____

Do you have a coach or a mentor to analyze your actions?

_____

_____

_____

_____

_____

_____

_____

_____

_____

_____

_____

_____

_____

_____

_____

_____

_____

_____

_____

_____

_____

_____

_____

Which actions seem possible?

_____

_____

_____

_____

_____

_____

_____

_____

_____

_____

_____

_____

_____

_____

_____

_____

_____

_____

_____

_____

_____

_____

_____

_____

_____

Talk about a big inspiring project that you are excited about:

_____

_____

_____

_____

_____

_____

_____

_____

_____

_____

_____

_____

_____

_____

_____

_____

_____

_____

_____

_____

_____

_____

_____

_____

_____

_____

_____

Chapter 9—Declare a New Future

This is how it is going to be:

_____

_____

_____

_____

_____

_____

_____

_____

_____

_____

_____

_____

_____

_____

_____

_____

_____

_____

_____

_____

This is my dream:

_____

_____

_____

_____

_____

_____

_____

_____

_____

_____

_____

_____

_____

_____

_____

_____

_____

_____

_____

_____

_____

_____

_____

This is how I envision it:

This is how I see, listen, and do clearly:

_____
_____
_____
_____
_____
_____
_____
_____
_____
_____
_____
_____
_____
_____
_____
_____
_____
_____
_____
_____
_____
_____
_____
_____
_____
_____

Say what is going to happen for you:

_____

_____

_____

_____

_____

_____

_____

_____

_____

_____

_____

_____

_____

_____

_____

_____

_____

_____

_____

_____

_____

_____

_____

_____

_____

This is the way it will be:

_____

_____

_____

_____

_____

_____

_____

_____

_____

_____

_____

_____

_____

_____

_____

_____

_____

_____

_____

_____

_____

_____

_____

What do you think might bring you great joy?

_____

_____

_____

_____

_____

_____

_____

_____

_____

_____

_____

_____

_____

_____

_____

_____

_____

_____

_____

_____

_____

_____

_____

_____

What is it that makes you uniquely you?

_____

_____

_____

_____

_____

_____

_____

_____

_____

_____

_____

_____

_____

_____

_____

_____

_____

_____

_____

_____

_____

_____

_____

What is the life of your dream?

_____

_____

_____

_____

_____

_____

_____

_____

_____

_____

_____

_____

_____

_____

_____

_____

_____

_____

_____

_____

_____

_____

_____

_____

_____

What would others say are your talents, distinctive competencies, and gifts are?

_____

_____

_____

_____

_____

_____

_____

_____

_____

_____

_____

_____

_____

_____

_____

_____

_____

_____

_____

_____

_____

_____

_____

_____

_____

What you think your talents, distinctive competencies, and gifts are?

_____

_____

_____

_____

_____

_____

_____

_____

_____

_____

_____

_____

_____

_____

_____

_____

_____

_____

_____

_____

_____

_____

_____

_____

_____

_____

What are the things you like doing most?

_____

_____

_____

_____

_____

_____

_____

_____

_____

_____

_____

_____

_____

_____

_____

_____

_____

_____

_____

_____

_____

_____

_____

_____

What things do you feel most strongly about?

_____
_____
_____
_____
_____
_____
_____
_____
_____
_____
_____
_____
_____
_____
_____
_____
_____
_____
_____
_____
_____
_____
_____
_____
_____
_____
_____

What are your favorite ways to express yourself?

_____

_____

_____

_____

_____

_____

_____

_____

_____

_____

_____

_____

_____

_____

_____

_____

_____

_____

_____

_____

_____

_____

_____

_____

_____

What would you like to experience during this lifetime?

_____

_____

_____

_____

_____

_____

_____

_____

_____

_____

_____

_____

_____

_____

_____

_____

_____

_____

_____

_____

_____

_____

_____

_____

_____

_____

_____

What is it you love?

_____

_____

_____

_____

_____

_____

_____

_____

_____

_____

_____

_____

_____

_____

_____

_____

_____

_____

_____

_____

_____

_____

_____

_____

_____

_____

_____

_____

What are you passionate about, even if you have no experience at it?

_____
_____
_____
_____
_____
_____
_____
_____
_____
_____
_____
_____
_____
_____
_____
_____
_____
_____
_____
_____
_____
_____
_____
_____

Are there any specific things you're interested in pursuing that light you up?

_____

_____

_____

_____

_____

_____

_____

_____

_____

_____

_____

_____

_____

_____

_____

_____

_____

_____

_____

_____

_____

_____

_____

_____

Pick a domain you like to work on.

_____

_____

_____

_____

_____

_____

_____

_____

_____

_____

_____

_____

_____

_____

_____

_____

_____

_____

_____

_____

_____

_____

_____

_____

_____

_____

_____

What you want to explore from the domain you have picked?

_____

_____

_____

_____

_____

_____

_____

_____

_____

_____

_____

_____

_____

_____

_____

_____

_____

_____

_____

_____

_____

_____

_____

_____

What is this domain for?

_____

_____

_____

_____

_____

_____

_____

_____

_____

_____

_____

_____

_____

_____

_____

_____

_____

_____

_____

_____

_____

_____

_____

_____

_____

What you can build from this domain?

_____

_____

_____

_____

_____

_____

_____

_____

_____

_____

_____

_____

_____

_____

_____

_____

_____

_____

_____

_____

_____

_____

_____

_____

_____

Chapter 10—Success is Just A Few Minutes Away

The magic key is: *"How to Be Super Organized"*

Everything in its place

Make sure you have a certain place for all your belongings and an easy access in time of need.

Avoid Clutter

Have a routine check-up on all your closets. If you don't need it, or have not used it, give it away. That way there will be a place for new things that are coming in.

Clean as you go

Put everything back in its place when finished with it. This way, the place always looks nice and neat. Then have a routine clean up at least once a week.

Plan ahead

Every night write down your "To Do" list. This will give you a clear action plan to lead you to accomplishment. If any of your goals didn't get finished, simply transfer them to tomorrow's list.

Create systems

It doesn't matter what kind as long as it works for you and you have an organized system.

Set priorities

Things that are important come first. This will make it easy for decision-making and saving time.

Separate the tasks

Keep a separate list of personal and work related tasks that you would like to achieve. Write down long-term goals and immediate ones. Then prioritize them so you can get them into the "To Do" list.

My plan of action to be organized:

_____

_____

_____

_____

_____

_____

_____

_____

_____

_____

_____

_____

_____

_____

_____

_____

_____

_____

_____

_____

_____

_____

_____

_____

_____

_____

SOLUTIONS

Tips to get you started

DAILY RUSH

Get a jumpstart the night before. Select yours and your children's outfits, see what the kids would like to have for breakfast, have lunch bags ready to go. This way will be way ahead of schedule. You can relax and enjoy quality time with your family.

Get up early, enjoy a cup of coffee or herbal tea and catch the daily news. This way you have time to get ready hassle-free.

MEAL PREPARATION

Every week make a list of daily menus and post it. Don't leave the grocery shopping to the last minute. Prepare ahead of time as much as you can. Then, when it is time to cook, you only need to put it together. Have healthy snacks handy for kids, hubby and yourself for an easy access. Make school lunches in the evening while preparing dinner. Have a good, nutritious selection of ready to go breakfast to choose from for a healthy daily start.

BLUE DAYS

No one is perfect. No one has the high energy levels all the time. Being organized is one of the keys to let you plan ahead and save time for you to be able to relax and take advantage of your days a bit more.

Being organized does not mean putting pressure on you, or to expect everything to be perfect.

We are human and naturally we get tired. Some days we have lower energy levels than usual. Try to relax and enjoy the day. You can relax no matter where you are or what you need to do.

Tips:

- Breathe deep every once in a while, close your eyes, bend your neck back, and relax the head.
- Massage your skin, arms, and neck, for better circulation.
- Always keep in mind that it can be done tomorrow.
- Never put pressure on yourself by rushing things.

Your health / fitness

Take your vitamins daily. Taking your vitamins will reduce the overall stress on your body.

Keep a regular exercise schedule for at least twice a week for 20-30 minutes

Personal time

Take time to care for and pamper yourself.

Remember to pencil time for yourself onto the calendar while you planning the family and career schedule for the week.

- Relax in with a hot bath Arrange for a good massage / once in a while
- Get together with friends and relax
- Make time to be alone

— Feeling burned out from work? Take a vacation, a day off, do nothing at all. You will be more productive the next day.

— Listen to your favorite music, or motivational tapes, while driving to work or between appointments.

— Make time to have a lunch or dinner alone with your loved one. Keep the romance around all the time.

— For your own sake, remember to say "NO" if you don't want to add something to your schedule. Whether it is on your personal time or any other projects that you have planned.

Hassle free holidays

— Plan ideas ahead of time, before each holidays or special occasion arrives.

— Make a list of gifts to save time when shopping.

— Get the family involved in cooking and craft projects. This way you get a chance for family bonding and less stress for you.

— Get greeting cards ahead of time. Complete them ahead of time. Mail them ahead of time. Then relax and enjoy time before the holidays arrive.

— Take advantage of catalog and shopping on **Internet***, save time.

— Keep parties simple and pleasant. Get other people involved and let them help you with the chores.

— If all the family members won't get along well one choice is to separate the guest and schedule the gatherings for different times.

---

*   Internet: There is a world of information out there. For a list of the best places to shop on Internet visit the **WorldGreatestMall.com**.

Discover Your True Passion in Life

In life, there are chores and responsibilities that we have to do. We have to learn to manage our life in a productive way, but never let that get you too far from your true passion in life.

To be able to have it all in life is to be able to stay close with your personality and your soul.

You have to capture:

— The connection with your personality and your soul's desire
— Connect with your passion in life
— Reawaken your soul's desire
— Listen to what you say to you
— Make time for yourself
— Meditate
— Devote your talents, skills, time, and love to all areas of the community to help
— Start uncovering what is important to you
— Always stay in touch with your true calling and purpose in life

Get to work

List 10-30 activities you love to do.

(List the things you like to do, not what your parents, society, friends, children, or your partner brought to you).

_____

_____

_____

_____

_____

_____

_____

_____

_____

_____

_____

_____

_____

_____

_____

_____

_____

_____

_____

_____

_____

_____

_____

Assignment:
Pick an activity and act upon it.

Write the whole process you went through:

_____

_____

_____

_____

_____

_____

_____

_____

_____

_____

_____

_____

_____

_____

_____

_____

_____

It is normal to see the road easier when you pick a domain that is familiar to you. It is also normal to face frustration when you are taking an unfamiliar road, unless you try and learn the skills of the trade. Take your time and concentrate on the possibilities.

Conversation for Possibilities

I dream, therefore, I am.
I am, therefore, I believe.
I believe, therefore, I can.
I know I can, because I try.
I try, because I seek, do, and want.
I want and I am going to have it all.

Learning to lead your life to the ultimate happiness is only a matter of having the right skills.

The right skills are the simple steps that you take to declare your victory.

Every time you take a step it is a major victory toward your life plan.

Start with your dream.

Lead your dream to your destiny.

There is nothing that can hold you back.

To have a happy life is to love your life.

You will love your life, because you worked so hard for it.

To love your life is to clean and polish it from inside and out.

The Ultimate Rules

Life is great, but it will bring an ultimate challenge for you to grow.

The life challenges are specifically designed for you to get you to your higher self.

The life challenges show their face to you as fear, anger, uncertainty, doubts, and more *when they encounter your weakness.*

The life challenges come to you as sickness, loss of a loved one, abusive childhood, success, failure, and more to *challenge your strength.*

The life challenges are here and no one is an exemption.

The only power you have is to be resourceful and find a way out to your advantage.

A way out is the law of concentrating on spiritual self. That everything happens to take us to our higher self, divine love, and abundance.

The Rules to Discover Your Dream Life

- You are here. Celebrate your life.
- Life is about living.
- Live to reach your higher self.
- Live for a better humanity.
- We are all part of a chain.
- You are very important.
- See yourself worthy, no matter where you are, and what you do.
- See all others as worthy, no matter who they are, and what they do.
- Life's challenges come to you to see yourself clearly.
- God wants you to be happy.
- Every good soul wants you to capture your dream.
- See the whole picture of life.
- There is a road and you are in it, cherish it.
- You have the choice to lead your life.
- The choice to fight back against the obstacles.
- The choice to learn.
- Learn the winning skills.
- Learn the solutions.
- Face your fears.
- The only way to win your dream is to see your fears clearly.
- See the road clearly.
- This road is going to have all seasons, mountains to climb, enemies to fight, allies to find, and more.
- Be patient and try to see the heart of the matter.
- Never let the swamp of sadness drag you down.

- Know and believe deep in your heart that there is always an answer.
- Believe in your heart that things always happen for a reason.
- See the reason of why you are, wherever you are.
- Find a greater solution in whatever you do.
- Find your passion in life for a better you.
- Help others in life for a better humanity.

You Become What You Think

Think Success...you become successful

Think Thin, Fit and Healthy...you become thin, fit and healthy

Think good friends...you'll have good friends

Think balance...you'll have balance

Think happy...you'll be happy

Think Rich...you'll be rich

Make a list of your own thoughts

_____

_____

_____

_____

_____

_____

_____

_____

_____

_____

_____

_____

_____

_____

_____

_____

_____

_____

_____

_____

_____

_____

_____

_____

What is Success?

Everyone is going to have a different definition of success. Success is the final frontier to find happiness, enjoyment, peace, and balance in all areas of your life.

What is the meaning of success to you?

_____

_____

_____

_____

SUCCESS

"The secret of success is to understand that, despite all of other responsibilities, the best time to begin is now."
Richard Carlson

"That some achieve great success, is proof to all that others can achieve it as well."
Abraham Lincoln

"People seldom see the halting and painful steps by which the most insignificant success is achieved."
Anne Sullivan

"The dictionary is the only place where success comes before work."
Mark Twain

"Do not let what you cannot do interfere with what you can do."
John Wooden

"Ones best success comes after their greatest disappointments."
Henry Ward Beecher

"The road to success is to try new things, take new risks, and face old fears."
Mera Lord

"If you're climbing the ladder of life, you go rung by rung, one step at a time. Don't look too far up, set your goals high but take one step at a time. Sometimes you don't think you're progressing until you step back and see how high you've really gone."
Donny Osmond

"Many a man has finally succeeded only because he has failed after repeated efforts. If he had never met defeat he would never have known any great victory."
Orison Swett Marden

"It's simply a matter of doing what you do best and not worrying about what the other fellow is going to do."
John R. Amos

"Thre is only one success—to be able to spend your life in your own way."
Christopher Morley

"Every person who wins in any undertaking must be willing to cut all sources of retreat. Only by doing so can one be sure of maintaining that state of mind known as a burning desire to win—essential to success."
Napoleon Hill

"Part of being successful is just hanging in there and sticking with it."
Unknown

"What would you attempt to do if you knew you would not fail?"
Robert Schuller

"Success seems to be largely a matter of hanging on after others have let go."
William Feather

"The gent who wakes up and finds himself a success hasn't been asleep."
Wilson Mizner

"I don't think you have to chase success, but you do need to slow down enough to let it catch up with you."
Richard Carlson

"Success usually comes to those who are too busy to be looking for it."
Henry David Thoreau

"The person who goes farthest is generally the one who is willing to do and dare. The sure-thing boat never gets far from shore."
Dale Carnegie

"People of mediocre ability sometimes achieve outstanding success because they don't know when to quit. Most men succeed because they are determined to."

George Allen

"If there is any one secret of success, it lies in the ability to get the other person's point of view and see things from that person's angle as well as from your own."

Henry Ford

"Success is doing what you want to do, when you want, where you want, with whom you want, as much as you want."

Anthony Robbins

"The most important single ingredient in the formula of success is knowing how to get along with people."

Theordore Roosevelt

"The ladder of success is never crowded at the top."

Napoleon Hill

"Success is the sum of small efforts, repeated day in and day out."

Robert Collier

"Just don't give up trying to do what you really want to do. Where there is love and inspiration, I don't think you can go wrong."

Ella Fitzgerald

"If you want to succeed you should strike out on new paths rather than travel the worn paths of accepted success."
John D. Rockefeller, Jr.

"Six essential qualities that are the key to success: Sincerity, personal integrity, humility, courtesy, wisdom, charity."
Dr. William Menninger

"Always bear in mind that your own resolution to success is more important than any other one thing."
Abraham Lincoln

"One person with a belief is equal to ninety-nine who have only interests."
John Stuart Mill

"Success is not the key to happiness. Happiness is the key to success. If you love what you are doing, you will be successful."
Albert Schweitzer

"In order to succeed, your desire for success should be greater than your fear of failure."
Bill Cosby

"I do not like to repeat successes, I like to go on to other things."
Walt Disney

"Men succeed when they realize that their failures are the preparation for their victories."
Ralph Waldo Emerson

"Flaming enthusiasm, backed by horse sense and persistence, is the quality that most frequently makes for success."
Dale Carnegie

"To become successful, it's critical to focus on what you can do, not on what you can't do."
Richard Carlson

"Do a little more each day than you think you possibly can."
Lowell Thomas

"There is no greatness without a passion to be great, whether it's the aspiration of an athlete or an artist, a parent, or a business person."
Anthony Robbins

"To succeed means that you may have to step out of line and march to the sound of your own drummer."
Keith Degreen

"Nothing happens until you make it happen."
Anonymous

"There is only one success—to be able to spend your life in your own way."
Christopher Morley

SUCCESS *by Ralph Waldo Emerson*

To laugh often and much;

To win the respect of intelligent people and the affection of children;

To earn the appreciation of honest critics and endure the betrayal of false friends;

To appreciate beauty,

To find the best in others,

To leave the world a bit better, whether by a healthy child, a garden patch or a redeemed social condition;

To know even one life has breathed easier because you have lived.

This is to have succeeded.

~ Ralph Waldo Emerson ~

Life is full of challenges, but it's interesting, thrilling, happy, and abundantly rewarding.

Best wishes to you all.

In search of total happiness

Total happiness can be reached and it will be yours to keep.

- *Find out what is really important to you and concentrate on it.*

- *Keep journals. Write down the things you would like to achieve*

- *Write down things in term of wants. I want to do this and that. I want to be here or there.*

- *Make decisions on the fact to get closer to your true desires. Everything starts with one step at a time and act as if it is there for you.*

- *Act on it as if it has already have happened. (Example: I want to be successful. Work on it little by little, step by step. While working to get where you want to be just say: I am successful. I am successful.)*

- *Finding a right balance with all the areas of family, career, children, health, fitness, friends, your past, and your future.*

- *Knowing what to do in daily life and long term plans of what you like to do, where you like to be in the near future, and long term future.*

List your thoughts and action plans.

_____
_____
_____
_____
_____
_____
_____
_____
_____
_____
_____
_____
_____
_____
_____
_____
_____
_____
_____
_____
_____
_____
_____
_____
_____
_____
_____

Conclusions

Make this book a journal to lead you in achieving your dream life. All you need to do is to fill in the blanks and turn your thoughts into actions.

This is a method to let you win your life over and over again. This is a workbook for finding your true self and analyzing your deepest dreams and desires from within and out.

You need to work on these matters throughout your life.

About the Author

Mera Lord is an author, psychologist, business consultant, image consultant, entrepreneur, producer, writer, director, and motivational speaker.

She has helped people, celebrities, and top executives to overcome their obstacles and roadblocks, and to achieve their dream life.

She strongly believes that you can achieve anything you want in life just by focusing on your desired lifestyle, by being resourceful, and by finding the right skills.

You can find these books written by the author:

I Weight No More

In Search of Answers

Millionaire's Workbook

The Lucky People

Recommended Web Sites to Visit

IWeightNoMore.com

This web site is created and maintained by the Author. For the latest information on weight loss, self-motivation and other books and conferences by the author visit this web site.

BzWoman.com

Provides help and guidance in variety of areas. You can also receive personal and confidential help by contacting Jenna (AskJenna) at BzWoman.com.

HowToStayYoung.com

Everything you want to know about living longer. Includes links to the latest developments in this area. Includes guidance on use of vitamins and herbs.

SuccessMotivationalInstitute.com

Need some motivation or enthusiasm, visit the Success Motivational Institute web site to get started.

MillionairesWorkbook.com

This site was created based on the success motivational book "Millionaire's Workbook". The author believes any one can be a millionaire. The book and the site help you find your own way to become rich.

Bibliography and Recommended Books

Gail Blanke, In My Wildest Dreams, Simon & Schuster Publishing, Incorporated / May 1998

Sheree Bykofsky, 500 Terrific Ideas for organizing everything, Galahad Books / March 1998

Jack Canfield and Mark Victor Hansen, Dare to Win, Berkley Publishing Group / January 1995

Susan Jeffers, Ph.D., Feel the Fear and do it Anyway, Fawcett Book Group / April 1996

M. Scott Peck, M.D., The Road Less Traveled, Simon & Schuster Trade / September 1997

Robert Schuller, Power Thoughts, achieve your true potential through power thinking, Zondervan Publishing House / October 1993

W. Clement Stone, The Success System that never fails, St. Martin's Press, Inc. / July 1989

Denis Waitley, The new dynamics of Goal setting, Morrow, William & Co / July 1996

0-595-20990-4